My Story...My Way

Living Life Full

Circle

My Story...My Way

Living Life Full

Circle

By

MARILYN DEAN

John Sheldon -
Thanks for your
support.
Be blessed!
xox
Marilyn Dean
10/19/2002

ISBN: 1-58721-445-8

This book is printed on acid free paper.

1stBooks-rev. 3/19/01

About The Book. . .

"My Story. . . My Way – Living Life Full Circle" is a book that explores, in depth, the series of events that we call life. It recognizes that the choices we make and the paths we trod do make a difference but, in the final analysis, we are who we are.

It is the wish of the author that each reader come to know the essence of who she is; God's child – unique, distinct and set apart. In addition, the reader will be lured into a better sense of self, encouraged by the honesty and simplicity of the book.

"My Story. . . My Way – Living Life Full Circle" is a labor of love that you will love.

BEYOND EXISTING

*"As I start my new circle,
I start happy – very, very happy."*

Sketch by: S. A. Morgan

"And this commandment have we from him, That he who loveth God love his brother also."

1 John: 5:21

Table of Contents

Dedicated to you. . .

to God – all the glory;

to my son and daughter, Ed and Roz, and my sister, Gwen – thanks and love now and forever;

to Sam – oodles of kudos; and

to Aunt Carrie – "hi!"

Acknowledgments

Acknowledgment to my son, Ed, for his encouragement to me to start this book. . .

Acknowledgment to my daughter, Roz, for holding my hand and lending her valued input. . .

And, to their Angels (in order of appearance), Brittney, Farrah, Kailyn, Imani and Kianna, for sitting still through "MaMoo's" songs and joining in my sing-a-longs.

Acknowledgments to my readers and listeners – Roz, Ed, Gwen, Sam, Coretta, Paul, Pat and family, David, Melvin and Linda, Sue and Sue, Rosetta, Barb, Charles and Willie, Lewis, Brad and Dee, Paulette and Edward. I would not have made it through without you. Your suggestions and encouragement were invaluable. . .

Acknowledgment to Paulette for her proof-reading skills and the time sacrificed to do it. . .

Acknowledgment to Sam for sharing with us "Certain Person" – for your input and inspiration – and for accepting me as I am. . .

Acknowledgment to Gwen for her continued excellence in editing, and for her undying patience and endurance through the retype, rewrite – retype, rewrite – and for being a true friend as well as a wonderful sister. . .

Acknowledgments to Rev. Henry E. Miller for the years of spiritual guidance before his death and to Elder Andrew D. Singleton, Jr., whose sermons and Bible study enlightened and inspired during the writing of this book. . .

And, acknowledgment to God for the gifts, family and friends.

FOREWORD

My Story. . . My Way
Living Life Full Circle

My Story. . . My Way – Living Life Full Circle was born out of a need to share the revelation that I'm alright and you're okay. Life, as we live it, is a series of events that culminate in a final product – final, but for only a second, for life is forever changing. The choices we make, the paths we trod, do make a difference. But, we are who we are.

My life consists not only of the expected peaks and valleys, but also of twists and turns, of fast forward and reverse, of falling and flying, of ecstasy and pain, of feast and famine, and of half moons and full circles.

I am all here in *My Story. . . My Way*, but in no particular order. My life's been lived in no particular order – other than Divine Order – predestined by God Almighty. I accept this – I accept God's Will in my life.

There was a time when I tried to change God's plan. I tried to talk more – I tried to move faster. I tried caring less, thinking I'd hurt less. I tried to be everything to everybody – martyring in leaving nothing for myself. I even tried changing my favorite color from green to peach. Then tried to figure out why.

I tried, and tried, and tried again until one day I just stopped. I didn't stop trying, I just stopped trying those nonsensical things that set me two steps forward and four steps back. I then tried something I do quite well but had forgotten – listening – listening to the still, sure voice of God reassuring me that He had made no mistake, that I am who I am because of the life He has given me. I am God's child – unique, distinct and set apart, and all for good purpose.

In listening, I learned that if the Lord God Almighty can love me – love me just as I am – love me just as He has molded me to be – then I best just love me too. And, I do. God's Word tells me to love you also. And, I do.

Yes, I am all here in *My Story. . . My Way*, and so are you. Maybe not all of you all the time, but you are here. Maybe not on page 30 today, but page 30 may be your pledge of allegiance tomorrow or, perhaps, your bridge to greener pastures this time next year. Time will tell.

Let us journey together in *My Story. . . My Way*. Just remember, your story – your way is in here too.

May the peace and love of God's still, sure voice bless you all.

Family

In today's society, the face of family <u>seems</u> to have taken on a new, expanded meaning. There is much rhetoric about this extended family; about step-mothers and step-fathers, step-brothers and step-sisters. Some folk even claim to have "play" relations – play "sons" and "daughters"; play "moms" and "pops"; play "aunts" and "uncles". But, believe me, family is no play thing. Then, there are those family members that happen to be measured in fractions, most often halves. Go figure.

In actuality, though, nothing has changed about family. True family never has been and never will be able to be defined in terms other than terms of the heart, of the soul, of the mind.

And, "What's blood got to do with it?" you ask. My answer – everything and nothing.

So, to <u>my family</u>, those who are etched in <u>my</u> heart, forever part of <u>my</u> soul, constantly inspiring <u>my</u> spirit mind, to you all – I commit my undying love.

God bless my family.

Certain Person

When you meet
your certain person
and don't know
it's like a smile
that don't show
it's like grievin'
and not feelin'
it's like hurtin'
and not healin'.

Sam A. Morgan

Time

Seems times is but
the whistling winds
blowing through
the hollow trees.
But time's the answer
to locked doors
for in time's hands
are all the keys. . .

To happiness,
progress and love –
to tragedy
and death, as well.
Want to know
what future brings?
Who knows,
for only time can tell!

Proem. . .

<u>*Self Portrait*</u>

"We all have different ways we would like others to perceive us . . . impressions, opinions, conclusions, as is life, are all based upon individual perceptions. It's interesting, though, how we perceive ourselves or how we want to be perceived."

<u>God Is. . .</u>

My tie that binds –
My rock that holds –
My light that shines –
My gift of love.

My heart made pure –
My fears unleashed –
My joy in living –
My inner peace.

He's my beginning –
He's my end –
And the wisdom to know. . .
Oh, yes –
Oh, yes –

God Is.

Proem. . .

On Friends

"There is a certain assurance with friends – an undeniable reliability that is unshakeable. Friendships can be tested, rocked, or tossed and turned, but when the dust settles and the shadows fade, all the consequential fallout will come down on the same side of the fence.

"Friends still."

Quiet Reassurance

Do I detect a solemn mood?
Did I just hear a long-drawn sigh?
You can't disguise your
troubled frown –
mustn't let life get you down.
Open the door and let me in –
Won't you tell me why?

You know,
two can make a load lighter –
can make a narrow road wider –
can brighten up a darkened path,
unbend a road,
remove the fork and
to the door be granted the key.
With all that is within me
to you I'll freely give.
Yes,
you can depend on me.

Time to quiet now,
Dear Precious One,
I just want to reiterate
that no matter, whatever,
life holds in store or things it may suggest,
you'll rise above that surging wave;
you'll make it through that torrent sea,
and you need not do it all alone,
for you'll always
have a friend in me.

Proem. . .

<u>*Missed Opportunity*</u>

"A love lost is not nearly as tragic as love unspoken. To let love embrace you and not embrace love back, to be courted by the look of love and not return the glance, to feel the warmth of love's glow then to snuff love's candle out, to be offered love's gift of peace to study war the more – is to treat love with indifference – is to break the heart of love – O, Sweet Love, oh, what a tragedy!"

<u>But I Never Said I Love You. . .</u>

From the times
I first remember,
I envied your strength and grace –
the warmth, the peace, the love
that forever was in your face.
I wanted, too, your inner glow,
but I never bothered
to tell you so.

I'd come, I'd look,
I'd listen in awe –
clinging to your every word –
nurturing my young mind –
never forgetting what I heard.
I wanted to tell you
but didn't, though –
now how I regret
not telling you so.

Your voice was like
an angel's whisper –
loving, kind and reassuring.
I took your existence so for granted –
felt your life forever enduring.
Where you were I wanted to go,
yet, you never knew
I loved you so.

But I Never Said I Love You. . .

Though God has taken
His angel home,
look down on me
and draw near.
Forgive me my silent tongue –
your voice gone;
now lend an ear
and believe me when I say to you
with God's good grace
we'll meet again.
I'll greet you with, "I love you" –
yes, I love you now
and I'll love you then.

Proem. . .

Words That Hurt

"Sticks and stones may break your bones. . . but words can break your heart.

"'I hate you!' These are the very last words I said to my brother before he went off to college. God knows that I didn't mean them, but God also knows that I did say them.

"How was I to know that we would never again meet, never again speak – no more hugging, laughing, no more caring or sharing?

"How could I have known when I thought death only came to other people's grandparents – not mothers, not fathers – and definitely not my brother?

"I didn't know then, but I surely know now. I also know that. . . sticks and stones can break my bones, but words have broken my heart.

"I'm sorry, Box."

Richard's Autumn

It has been a long,
long summer this season –
nineteen full years long.
Autumn has regretfully come –
pretty leaves dying one by one.

Many leaves gracefully falling,
a blanket for the ground below –
soon to be blown wistfully by;
many others to take their place.

A leaf is like a man,
you know,
on the tree of life,
accepting his charge
'till beckoned up home –
none other to take his place.

The leaf will soon be forgotten –
the man, of course, will not.
Living on in the minds of men,
leaving his mark on life.

Yes, God works in mysterious ways,
so I'll question not –
Just waiting for the winds to blow
and sever me from
the tree of life.

Proem. . .

<u>*Sacred Vows*</u>

"Our vows stated before God and man should be constantly restated within our hearts and continually reflected in our deeds.

"Hallowed then be the union.   Permanent then be the bond."

With Every New Day's Dawning

Just to have a new day dawn
is enough reaffirmation
that our lives were meant to be,
for you've been my inspiration
to take the next step,
add another mile,
breathe another breath.
You'd taken an existence
consisting only of hollows and voids
and developed it into a life –
complete with light and substance.

You've made my cup
to runneth over,
and do believe,
that I'm as grateful for the overflow
as for the necessities.

Yes, I may be a maudlin,
but of that you must not razz
for I'm one who knows that
that I have is what I've always wanted –
is all I'll ever need.
'Tis stated not for boasting's sake
but's my stronghold to keeping our vows mere.

With Every New Day's Dawning

So let's take this life
bestowed upon us
and continue as in the past –
hand in hand,
bound as one,
forever, together to stand –
steadfast in God's Will
no matter our circumstance.
This, My Love. . .
with every new day's dawning.

Proem. . .

<u>*Liquidating Loneliness*</u>

"To some, the word lonely is a bad word – a sentence of solitary confinement that can cripple you both physically and emotionally – and it can, if you let it. But don't.

"Take this lemon of longing and make yourself some lemonade. And, if it tastes a bit too tart, add dabs of self-esteem – little by little – until its flavor and palatability are just right."

That Constant Reminder

Pressing your lips to a mirror
can't take away the loneliness –
won't rid you of the emptiness
or obliterate your envy
of those who come in pairs.
Just reminds you where you stand,
at best,
when you are all you've got.

Independence can be a fine virtue
but liberation's a futility creed
when it strips of all that you need,
and surely when to masturbate
is the only
love-making on the slate
and when peaked
is only second rate,
you'd gladly take that back seat place,
when you are all you've got.

True-to-life self-image reflections can
remind you clearly where you stand
when you are all you've got.

Proem. . .

<u>*Grace Sufficient*</u>

"What do you do – what do you say, when all of your suspicions have been confirmed?

"How devastating to be forced to accept that the lipstick on his collar did not belong to Aunt Sue. How foolish to have risen to get aspirin for his headache when all that was wanted was a 'do not disturb' sign. Perhaps the birthday lingerie charged at Victoria's Secret was not stolen from the car.

"And, those periodic telephone one-rings? More likely signals, not mechanical malfunctions.

"You may ask yourself over and over and over, 'If it wasn't the truth, then was it a lie?' 'If it wasn't all truth, what part was a lie?' 'If partly a lie, was that lie you?'

"From peace to insanity – from maternity to paternity suit – what a ride. . . what a ride!

"Eventually, though, your mind will be freed, frustrations will wane, and your way will become crystal clear. Until then. . . What do you? What do you say?

"Just stand!

"God's Grace was sufficient for me."

From Trash to Treasure

Foolish is the man
who'll let life's only treasure
slip away for the thrill of a
one night's pleasure –
a loss he'll not recover,
that's too massive to measure.

Frustrated is the man
who will suddenly find
that the thrill of the night
was a play on his mind.
Then to cop a plea
with promises to refrain
and wonder why
he's still out in the rain,
is too much of a strain
on his inundated brain.

But, wise is the man who'll
check his neighbor's trash –
with a smile on his face,
deriving much pleasure –
for he knows
he may find his life's only true treasure –
a gift to protect
that's too precious to measure.

Proem. . .

Stripped

"It's a real heartbreaker when it happens to you. When the thieves come to your house, when they help themselves to your possessions – the "things" accumulated as a result of years of your hard work and your sacrifices – what an outrage – what a disappointment.

"It's not necessarily the "things" stolen which disappoints you so; rather, it's the dwarfed dreams, the tarnished values, the diminished faith in your fellow man.

"But, to add insult to injury, is to have the thieves be kin, blood, family. This, to me, goes beyond disappointment, it's utter disbelief – total heartbreak.

"And, you're hurt especially so when you know that they know that all they had to do was ask.

"It's at this point that one's ability to truly forgive is truly put to the test."

Dear "Brother"

It's not just Black on Black
but it's kin on kin
that make these ripoffs such a sin.
To have your "brother" break and take that
that you have worked to make
is surely a sin,
in anyone's namesake.

Shouldn't be Black for Black
but just human pride that
makes you dare not step aside,
for when your "sisters" need a hand
don't turn your back –
do what you can.
Get your act together,
Black Man.

Don't point your uppity
Black finger and say you'll
never again come this way.
Who knows,
for soon you might possibly be
just day-to-day making it
just like me.
My pride in myself you can
never destroy, but
in trying, you've gone from
Black Man to
plain boy!

Dear "Brother"

Is it clear?
Do you comprehend?
You make me shame to be your sister, Mister.
Must I repeat?
Do you understand?
I said,
"Get your act together,
Black Man!"

Proem. . .

My Personal Best

"Some folk, through no choice of ours and no choice of theirs, come into our lives leaving an indelible mark, one never to be effaced. The real time spent may be of short duration or for decades, but the impact will last forever.

"No one has expressed this better than songster Gladys Knight, when she passionately and soulfully sings. . .

> *'If anyone should ever write*
> *my life's story –*
> *For whatever reason*
> *there might be –*
> *You'll be there between each line*
> *of pain and glory –*
> *'Cause you're the best thing*
> *that ever happened to me.'*

"You, Pumpkin, are the best."

For You Only

Who needs love
for taking care of a need's sake?
That's dead!
I want love for love's sake.
I want your love.
I want to make love to you,
tenderly and totally;
that's living – I want to live!

Where to spend our time
is not the question.
The question is how.
Just walking, needing, feeling,
talking, blending, kneeling;
just so it's together.
Don't you agree?

You know,
distance matters not
for you are always in my thoughts,
day in – day out.
Warm thoughts that comfort me
when time or miles interrupt
the harmony of our love.
Believe me –
distance matters not.

For You Only

A world of you and I
is more than sufficient –
it's totality.
We neither need not want for more.
The highness of our love
touches the sky.
It's infinity, Love, infinity.

And, trust!
What can I say –
it comes without asking.
There are no doubts,
there are no regrets.
It's just you and me confiding, relying.
Trust!
There are no doubts.

There is no you then me –
just you and me.
We as one, together,
living our lives inseparable –
wanting it always to be that way.
We as one together,
always.

These things I say, My Love,
are for you only.

Proem. . .

<u>*Words Of Love*</u>

"God"

"unconditional"

"committed"

"forever"

"priceless"

"true"

"selfless"

"peace"

"God"

A Mother's Love

There's nothing like a Mother's love,
the time she takes –
the things she'll do –
the problems that she'll help you through.
With the wisdom
to tell you when you're wrong –
puts you out of grace,
but not for long.

With a heart of gold
like you've never dreamed of. . .
No, there's nothing like a Mother's love.

There's nothing like a Mother who
provides life's "special"
cares for you. . .
Will hug you when you need a hug –
will teach you
of God's merciful love.
Can mend a heart and dry a tear
and this she'll do
year after year. . .
Giving heart and soul for her family.
Yes, a Mother's love is the epitome.

With a heart of gold
like you've never dreamed of. . .
No, there's nothing like a Mother's love.

Proem. . .

<u>*Overwhelmed*</u>

"At times we catch it from all sides — nothing seems to be going right — too many problems, too much work, too little money, not enough time; sleepless nights, traffic jams, wayward children, sickness; heart broken, spirit broken, car won't start on a bad hair day.

"But, in the midst of it all, as the clouds are lowered and the fog rolls in, remember:

> *': but God is faithful, who will not suffer you to be tempted above that ye are able; but will with the temptation also make a way to escape, that ye may be able to bear it.'*
> *1 Cor. — 10:39*

"Then, as promised, watch the clouds lift and the fog recede — the emptied vessel before the fountain, once again refilled."

Trapped

Surrounded –
surrounded by six
blank, doorless walls
no entry
no exit signs in sight
my hands are tied
my feet are bound
my mind's entrapped by day-to-day trivia
that's no longer trivia
but's monumental mole hills too steep to climb.

Avalanche –
life's an avalanche
rocks, hot lava
piling, piling
work and worry
higher, higher
there's no way to dig through this continuous slide
there is no coming out on top
there is no other side.

Falling –
please help
I'm falling
crushed – I'm being crushed
flashbacks, hallucinations
loud voices fill my head
abstract objects, indistinguishable sounds.

When I'll hit bottom – I just don't know.

If I'll hit bottom – I don't want to know.

Proem. . .

Broken Vessel

"Picture this. It's the day after Christmas, the hustle and bustle of the Season is winding down and you're alone. Really alone. The sigh you release that you think will bring relief – doesn't. It brings forth tears. You're not just alone – you're lonely. You're not just lonely – you're tired. You're not just tired – you're broken.

"It seems you've run out of energy, out of patience, out of time, out of breath. Reason escapes you and logic just left.

"You wonder – if you are your brother's keeper, then who will it be that keeps you?"

O, Life!

O, Life,
send me someone who'll let me once be weak,
who'll lead the way for me to follow –
lift me up if I should falter,
if I to err, they to alter –
'tis truly a need, so truly I seek –
O, Life, send me someone
who'll let me once be weak.

O, Life,
strength is a virtue that no one can deny
but I seek weakness and some ask why –
'cause there's strength
in the ability to absorb and recoup,
but like winter to spring I need time to regroup –
to regain my humility, my respect,
to be meek –
O, Life, send me someone
who'll let me once be weak.

O, Life,
this weakness I ask I want only to borrow –
if granted this wisdom I'll not keep it for long;
just time enough to draw upon its power
for myself and others who may need to lean on –
'tis truly a need, so truly I seek –
O, Life, send me someone
who'll let me once be weak.

Proem. . .

No Excuses Acceptable

"Many excuses are just spears thrown out that do nothing but insult the intelligence.

"Please don't insult my intelligence. You are too intelligent for that."

You Know Better

no excuses
no reasons
no exonerating yourself
you're at fault
we're ashamed
you get no absolution

how could you
what possessed you
to cross life's white line
how loathsome
this deep, dark abyss
you have broken God's own heart

take a stand
be a man
plead guilty to your senseless act
don't bore us
with your troubled past
we grant no pardons here

undeliverable
return to sender
this pathetic apology letter
one time too many
ten times too long
unforgiven
cause you know better

Proem. . .

<u>*Can't Nothin' Or Nobody*</u>

"What a real good feeling to know that you are where you want to be, you have what you need, that the only way is up, that it's full speed ahead and that no outside forces can halt or hinder this fiery ball of inertia.

"You stand on your vows, you believe in God's promise – 'What therefore God hath joined together, let no man put asunder.'

"Love conquers all. O, Love, victorious!"

Ain't No Danger

To deny myself
water when I thirst,
food when I hunger,
sleep when my body reeks with
exhaustion?
To deny me you?

Ain't no danger.

Why take the light of my life
and plunge
myself into total darkness,
knowing darkness is the proverbial
unfertile egg;
when you and I can grow
from seed to harvest?
Me to blow out the candle that
has brightened the path of my
every way?

Ain't no danger.

'Twould be foolish
to take that which has taken me
from the dungeons of despondency
to the height of ecstasy
and let go like the limbs of
Autumn
let go her leaves.

Ain't No Danger

To sever myself from you like the
amputation of a pianist's hands
and expect me not to even bleed?
Unthinkable.
Relax.

Ain't no danger.

For us it will be
to the peak of mountains,
to the depth of valleys,
to the edge of the oceans,
riding the waves of life
together.
Wet, wild, tousled, free.
Held only by that which binds our
two inner selves.
Then submerged – to emerge,
twisted, entwined,
molded – hard and firm
but now as an eternal one.
I to try and unmaster this perfect web?

Ain't no danger.

Danger enters
only when you will choose,
when you will have made that
fatal decision
to take that which you have
created,

Ain't No Danger

and in some fleeting instant take
away the breath of my life,
the core of my soul,
the beat of my heart –
to send me from young to old.
This only you can do –
I have neither the power nor
desire.

Rest assured, My Precious,
for ours is an indestructible
lifetime monument.
As will forever be
the peace of God,
birth and death,
black and white,
the sun and moon,
the water and the trees,
forever will be you and me.

For us to part?
I pledge to you –
never, never –

Ain't no danger.

Proem. . .

First Born

"What an exciting time!

"You wait with much anticipation for your baby's birth. You watch your body change in ways that seem miraculous, and you feel your mind racing with the thrill of it all. Wow! You're going to be a mother. . . another human's parent – a nurturer, a guide, a teacher, a counselor. So many new titles – such awesome responsibilities. You realize, though, that you have never been here, and you have never done this. The fact is. . . you just don't have a clue.

"Fear not. This chapter in time you'll master as you've mastered times before. . . with prayer and supplication. The ever-present, open arms of God awaits you and your child. What peace, what blessed assurance.

"Thank you, God."

My Little Man

Six,
And already he's a man –
Young and energetic,
Walking tall,
Frightened of nothing –
Reaching for it all.
Only six –
And he's My Little Man.

He reads of bears and
Rocket ships –
Of Dr. King and Superman –
Of phantoms in the ocean blue –
Of racing cars and of God on high.

He reads of it all
And he'll have it all.
That's the way it should be and
That's the way it's going to be for
My Little Man.

He'll forever retain his
Inquisitiveness –
Grow in his quest
And thirst for knowledge –
Ahead of today and into tomorrow –
Encompassing it all.

My Little Man

But, he'll have a heart
With room for love –
Compassion for the world at-large,
And be strong enough
When hurt to cry –
He'll be a well-rounded man.

But,
There will come a time
One day
When this little man of mine
Will go off into the world
Me thinking I'm being left behind. . .

But to him I'll always be Mommy. . .

And whether it's
Peace he's bringing to the world –
Pollution
Removing from the air –
Reviving
The dead after death –
Or having a wife and child of his own,
He knows he can always call here home.

Reluctantly,
But with faith in he,
I'll let the man go.

My Little Man

Six,
And already he's a man –
Young and energetic,
Walking tall,
Frightened of nothing;
Reaching for it all.
Only six –
But, forever, My Little Man.

Proem. . .

More Than Gray Matter

"The mind is a powerful instrument which allows us to develop perceptions and process reason. Our minds are where our views and opinions are formulated – where creativity is born – where defenses are devised and where healing begins and forgiving ends.

"The very thought of such power is overwhelming.

"Just think about it."

The Thought of You

The thought of you
is like a protective coating
that embraces and shields me
from all things and all persons
who may want to hurt or harm me.

I feel with you in my life,
the world is mine. . .
be it mine –
I give it you,
for you, My Love,
deserve it in its entirety.

You're deserving of its sun, its moon, its stars,
its clouds, its joy, its laughter and,
of course, its love. . .

Its sun because your radiance energizes me. . .
its moon because the warmth of your being comforts me. . .
its stars for you forever keep that twinkle in my eyes. . .
its clouds for it's you who soothes my pain. . .
its joy because you make my soul to sing. . .
its laughter because you truly have made me happy. . .
and its love because you are love
and because I love you.

This, My Love, and much, much more. . .

With just the thought of you.

Proem. . .

<u>Different Means Different</u>

"We, as human beings, are constantly changing. Change can be a good thing. Just imagine living from year to year and not knowing any more about life this year than last year. Just suppose you are stricken with illness and because change leaves, the illness cannot. The very thought sickens me. Change can be the means to an end. . . the answer to the problem. . . our calm after the storm.

"Now, if you're one of those people who views change in a negative light then, perhaps, I've been able to change your mind.

"Change can be a good thing."

You, I And The Butterfly

You and I are very much like a butterfly. . .

We're an expression of beauty
whose lives intertwine, linked
by mesmerizing hues that radiate
as from a post-storm rainbow. . .

We're a touching of body to soul
that mystically unlocks
the enigma of midnight
and captures the effulgence and
magic of moonlight. . .

We're that symbol of metamorphic change
that when unveiled
reveals a flawless simplicity
of strength of mind
over that which does not matter. . .

You and I, we're very much like a butterfly.

Though transformed we may be,
we're immortalized in memory –
just having to close our eyes
to recapture our place in the skies. . .

Yes,
You, I and the Butterfly.

Proem. . .

A Spade's A Spade

"Have you ever experienced the hypocrisy of a feigned relationship – of a relationship that has boundaries steeped in insincerity and intolerance?

"Particularly, when we speak of so-called 'friendships' we must be very careful. Because, if we can work together, shop together, laugh, cry and grieve together. . . sometime – but can never live together, worship together or have your daughter marry my son. . . ever; then, there is something terribly wrong with this picture.

"Many may call this prejudice or judgmental or bias or bigotry, but I call it ignorance – ignorant and unbelieving of the fact that we are all God's children and unaccepting of the precept that we love one another as God loves us.

"It really is ignorant."

Where Friendship Draws The Line

If I can't sit down
next to you
anytime, anywhere, anyplace,
then I'll not sit
anywhere with you –
try to understand
my pride.

If I can't move
right next to you
and not have you
want to run,
then I'll stay right here where I be
and be happy
in my dignity.

If I can't kneel
down next to you
and worship our Lord on cross,
then there's nothing to do
but pray for you –
a soul completely lost.

For true believers know
God doth not measure
in wealth,
color or intelligence,
and that God doth know our inner minds
and rewards
accordingly.

<u>Where Friendship Draws The Line</u>

So accept
whatever life gives
and your just rewards
open-handedly,
and I'll stay right here where I be
and be happy
in my dignity.

Proem. . .

No One Else Will Do

"It's simply amazing. . .

"when you know that you know, that you really, really know that your prayers have been answered and your heart has been healed. . .

"that your knight in shining armor, that the captain of your seas – that this man among men who's been sent and blessed by God. . .

"who now overruns your hope cup, who now calms your doubts and fears – who patiently awaits you, who now shares your joyful tears;

"a God-send – tried and true. . .

"you now know that you know, that you really, really know, that. . .

"no one else will do!"

In Your Presence. . .

I dream of clear, calm, cloudless days
Of sultry, moonlit nights. . .
Of years gone by – of things to be
Of mountain peaks and roaring seas
Of life and death – of you and me –
All while In Your Presence.

You've touched my heart profoundly
In ways I never knew. . .
My heart now beats a happy tune
My heart has learned to smile
My heart doth gleam – yes, my heart sings –
In Your Presence all the while.

Your spirit is my spirit
A mate to bless my soul. . .
Our spirit soars on wings of grace –
In our spirit hope abounds
A spirit sate in joy and peace –
In Your Presence true love be found.

We'll be guided by our spirit
We'll survive on dreams fulfilled
Two hearts to share life's love with care. . .

In Your Presence –
In God's Will.

Proem. . .

<u>*Lasting Impressions*</u>

"At any given moment, one never knows who may be watching. Therefore, we should be always mindful of what we do (our actions) and what we say (our tongues). Young eyes and ears, children's eyes and ears in particular, take in images and sounds that can be devastating and long-lasting. So, in order to be responsible and accountable to our young (and each other), we must ensure that our actions and words remain consistently respectful to them and to ourselves.

"Ultimately, know and believe that God knows all hearts."

Peek and Boo

What do you think
of a woman
who sleeps with men
in cars
whose character
is in question
whose morals are ajar?

I
try
not
to

.

Proem. . .

The Beast of Deception

"There is no justification to wrong. By virtue of its definition: not what ought to be; not according to rule; any injury, hurt, pain or damage; to treat with injustice; to go awry – wrong is not right and you're not right when you commit wrong.

"There is no rationalizing – not revenge, not payback, not spite, nor retaliation – you must do unto others as you would have had them do unto you."

Never More

To be able to offer
only part of the life
of another man's wife
just wouldn't be right,
for you, Sweetheart,
deserve much more.
So, in order to even the score –
to prove my love,
I'll see you
never more.

I did not plan to have it end
and I love you too much
just to be your friend.
Though my body reeks
with pain galore,
I'll turn my back,
close my eyes
and see you
never more.

But I'll remember that misty morn,
those love-filled nights,
and the park swings
where we reached our height.
You, my darling,
I truly adore,
and to prove this love,
like magic you came,
like magic I'll leave.
And I'll see you
never more.

Proem. . .

<u>*Gentle Persuasion*</u>

"When speaking of love, one should not find it necessary to convince another to love, nor to define love. . . a loving heart knows love.

"Surely, we analyze and, at times, try to rationalize our love. . . but, perhaps that is as far as it should go. Perhaps, being able to sort out one's own feelings is about the best for which one should hope.

"At the least, one's mate should be accepting of the gift of your love and decide, independent from any gentle, friendly persuasion what to offer, if anything, in return.

"The resultant truth is a truth on which sound decisions can be made.

"The bottom line? You cannot manufacture love!"

And Still You Don't Respect Me

You say I am the world's best wife
And that you love me dearly.
You say I am what makes your life –
But, still you don't respect me.

I make you feel just like a king
With crown and throne and all.
You say I make your heart to sing –
And, still you don't respect me.

I try my best not to complain
Of the many nights alone.
I do without and bear the pain –
Yet, still you don't respect me.

I warn you, yes, you know I do;
For I want our "love" to last
And so, My Dear, I beg of you –
Please show me some respect!

Proem. . .

Testimony

"I remember. I'll always remember the clear, confident doctor's voice lamenting my prognosis – forecasting an overcast life of limitations and restrictions – diagnosing 'childless.'

> " 'she won't. . .
> she can't. . .
> she mustn't. . .
>
> " 'be careful. . .
> be cautious. . .
> be wary. . .
>
> " 'don't try. . .
> don't assert. . .
> don't insist. . .'

"The textbooks warned – no; but God said yes!

"Yes, motherhood, to me, is an extra special blessing."

A Mother's Prayer

Dear Lord,

Years ago You answered a prayer and gave to me one precious son and one precious daughter.

Through infancy and childhood and, above all, through their teens, I prayed and You answered. I knelt in the midnight hour and at the dawn of many days, asking Your **courage** to seek out the future, Your **strength** to weather the storms, Your **hope** for a brighter tomorrow, Your **faith** just to continue, and Your **love** to span the gaps. "Ask and it shall be given" – I asked, You gave – and now I thank You, Lord.

I asked for courage and I saw her fears subside – she sprouted up, developed a bud, and blossomed into a vibrant, fragrant, ever-blooming rose. I asked for strength and I saw his weaknesses fade – he flexed and stretched and where a boy stood now a man stands. For this, I thank You, Lord.

I ask today, Lord, for knowledge. Let them both know that whomever they are or will ever be, whatever they know or will acquire, or whatever they have or will accumulate, it all comes from You. Grant them the knowledge of the power of prayer, the knowledge of the gift of love, and the knowledge that, in time, You will grant them wisdom.

Continue, Lord, to love, protect and guide them.

Your Humble Servant,
"Their Mother"

Proem. . .

<u>Enabling</u>

"Ignorance is bliss, you say? I don't think so. Not always, anyway.

"To allow a plague, a vicious cycle to permeate your sphere of peace – whether knowingly or unknowingly – has its price tag.

"The toll we pay for turning our backs, closing our eyes, and ducking our heads into sinking sand just might add up to be life's bottom line called 'no other choice' – no other choice but to walk away."

Sign Of The Times

Why I bother to work?

When I think I could choke. . .

to help support

the thieves,

to clad me

in rags,

and to keep you

in "smoke" and "coke"!

Proem. . .

<u>***Bo Jangling***</u>

"There is no tap dancing around pain without someone being hurt."

What Now?

After all our trials of late –
the shattered hopes
and broken hearts –
the circumstance that made us part. . .
our coming to grips with reality –
the realization of our destiny –
to ask what I must is insanity!
But ask I must,
"What now?"

For a man to tune in on my needs
all he must do
is plant the seeds
to compassion, respect and loyalty.
Yes, love is grand,
save love cannot stand alone.
But, now's too late, I've gone that extra mile
with a tear in my eye –
face void of smile.
Our road did more than simply bend,
'twas detour, detour,
dead end.
Another journey?
Never again!
So the question remains,
"What now?"

What Now?

Making this final decision to act
has taken a load
off my back,
but I won't let the past ruin me –
to sulk and hate can be agony,
so I'll not regret nor compare –
just mend this heart and be prepared,
for I've learned it hurts when you truly care. . .

"What Now?"

Proem. . .

Renewed Awareness

"How amazing. . . that when love notices you, you notice love. . . how love's sweet smell lingers; how you see love on each face; how you hear love in the wind; how you're touched by love's embrace – O, taste of love, O, taste of life!

"Oh, how amazing!"

Have You Noticed?

Have you noticed –

> The beauty of the days
> The stillness of the nights
>
> The laughter of the children
> The wisdom of the old?

Have you noticed –

> The swaying of the trees
> The gentleness of the breeze
>
> The water is much wetter
> And runs a whole lot deeper?

Have you noticed –

> The giggle in **my** voice
> The power of **your** smile
>
> The strength of shedded tears
> The blending of **our** years?

Have you noticed–

> The beating of the drums
> The love in the love song
>
> That my heart is in your hands
> That I'm glad that I am?

Have you noticed?

> I have!

Proem. . .

<u>*At First Sight*</u>

"If it's truly love, it can't be soon enough!"

<u>Smitten</u>

Too soon
to
be
love;
too sweet
to
be
lust!

Proem. . .

<u>*Just A Statistic*</u>

"We've all read about it – the rising number of single-parent homes – homes for the most part headed by women. Many of these women – our mothers – have awesome responsibilities that, at times, overwhelm them. Some mothers are so bombarded by just the day-to-day necessities of food, clothing and shelter that little energy is left for much else. Foolishly, they try to give their children the sense that they can "do it all" – be both parents – mother and father.

"In time, though, after repeated, futile attempts to play this double role, it becomes apparent that they're attempting the impossible, that they've succeeded only in spreading themselves too thin, creating a mother for their children with a hole in her soul – wounded and weary.

"Instead of trying to play this dual role, it's far wiser for mothers to strive to be the best of who they truly are. With God as their help and strength – just be mother. For, when all else fails and all others fade, a mother's love prevails.

"Thank God for our mother's love."

Absentee Dad

I always knew where he lived
Always knew right where he worked
I *heard* that he could really preach
But, I never knew the man.

He never blessed *our* table
Never led *his own* in prayer
How could he – he was never there
No, I never knew this man.

I look just like his sister
I'm short just like his mom
Whene'er we met, I *called* him Dad
Though, I never knew the man.

I remember the things he *never* said
Remember the times he *never* came
I know we have the same last name
But, I never knew the man.

He never *saw* me graduate
Never *heard* my nighttime cries
Never once did he dry my eyes
No, I never knew the man.

Was introduced *to* his daughter
But, not introduced *as* his daughter
Felt much like scalding water
No, I never knew this man.

Absentee Dad

When he died they all came
When he died they all acclaimed
Their condolences to our *family*
But, we never knew the man.

It's *hard* for me to understand
Hard to understand how I can
Have his eyes, his wit and his pink bottom lip
Yet, I never knew the man.

No, I never knew this man
'Tis plain for God and all to see
But the true tragedy is that
He *never, never, ever* knew me.

Proem. . .

My God And Me

In the early, early morning
before the world gets on its way,
I bow my knees and ask the Lord,
Lord, help me through this day.

I ask my God to guide me and
He says just do obey and
He will be my strength and light
each step along the way.

I pray to God to cleanse my heart
and He cautions me on pride – He says
take His love into my heart and
there He will abide.

So, I seek
God in my every walk,
God in my work,
God in my play, and
God in my talk.

And He says go forth my child in Me
and be the child that I would have you to be.

So, at the end of the day
when twilight hath come,
I thank God for His guidance,
for His mercy and His love.

Then I end the day as it began,
again on bended knee,
so, tomorrow I can face this world –
just my God and me.

Proem. . .

Braggadocio

"Many men who boast of their deeds or abilities or conquests do so mostly to deaf ears. People aren't really interested in listening to their incessant half-truths, and grossly over exaggerated tall tales. While they are recounting the 'how' of the notches in their belts, we onlookers stare openly at the insecurities worn so pathetically on their sleeves.

"It's sad, really."

Macho Man

I'm a man!
I'm a man!
Shouted he.

I can whip them;
I can beat them;
I can love them;
I can leave them!

I'm a man!
I'm a man!
Shouted he.

Ever young;
Never old;
Never shy;
Always bold!

I'm a man!
I'm a man!
Shouted he.

I'm exciting;
I'm inviting;
I'm untiring;
All inspiring!

Macho Man

I'm a man!
I'm a man!
Shouted he.

I take short ones;
I take tall ones;
Guess what?
I take all ones!

I'm a man!
I'm a man!
Shouted he.

I'll take a quickie
Or a long one.
I'm the king;
Oh, hear me sing!

I'm a man!
I'm a man!
Aren't I?

Proem. . .

<u>My Girl</u>

"Sugar and spice and everything nice. And, I do mean everything.

"From her Kodak smile to her girlish pout; from her independent nature to her strong family ties; from her unshakeable opinions to her willingness to listen; from her stubborn streak to her open sensitivity; from her last minute chaos to her voice of calm and reason; from her lows to her highs; from her ins to her outs; from her sense of timing to her lack thereof – yes, I do mean everything!

"I wouldn't trade a thing – wouldn't change a thing. . . for she's my sugar, she's my spice, she's life's everything nice.

"She's my girl."

My Daughter, My Sweet

As you laid inside my womb
cradled in your nest
my heartbeat sang you lullabies
sweet melodies a'humming
blessed our eternal bond
blessed the tie that binds
me to you
you to me
My Daughter, My Sweet.

I see it still, your tiny hand
reaching out in innocence
hungering to be fed of life
so willing to be led –
basking in life's sunlight
wishing on its star –
I marveled at this glory –
at last! a little me. . .
My Daughter, My Sweet.

I watched you as you listened
as you learned the laws of life. . .
golden is the rule –
precious are its gifts –
you are your brother's keeper –
and God's love never fails;
eager with this knowledge –
anxious just to see, you asked,
"What will I do, Mommy?"
"What will I be?"

My Daughter, My Sweet

Just you be you, My Angel Girl,
My Daughter, My Sweet.

My Daughter, you're a woman now
with angels of your own –
a consummate lady –
majestic, proud and strong.
You are my heart
you are my love
this love forever to be. . .
My Daughter, My Friend –
My Daughter, My Sweet.

Proem. . .

Making Love

"True lovemaking crescendo's not into the finality of climax, but bursts forth with the ebb and tide of many new beginnings – a constant rekindling of two virgin hearts expressing their gratitude."

An Awakening

I have found
one does not make love –
love is to be lived.

I have found
every time I truly love –
I live my love with you.

To have you quench my love-dry abyss
by being lulled
to a state of near unconsciousness
by the rhythmic spurt of repeated
orgasmic volcanic eruptions
which simultaneously
pierce through and arouse
my every nerve ending
will be, My Love,
the height and unsullied joy of our living.

I have found
true love
is born of life given –
not created for the making.

Proem. . .

<u>Chance Meeting</u>

"Sometimes, we are more than just two ships that pass in the night. Sometimes, we dock, layover, and explore this meeting of chance.   Then, we sail out – sailing out in separate ways – destinations unknown.

"By chance, yes.

"Regrets, no."

Brief Encounter

Memories are treasures –
heirlooms
to keep forever.
But when all
we have is a memory
it's hard to relate
to reality.
For, we've not just the
need to be needed
but, too, we
want to be wanted –
no longer to live the lie
of some storybook rhyme.
So, like all fairy tales,
we were
once upon a time.

Proem. . .

<u>Seizing The Opportunity</u>

"By clothing ourselves daily in the whole armor of God, we ready ourselves for victory – capable and unafraid to stand against the wiles of the world.

"Each new day is no accident – no stroke of luck – but is the miracle of God, granting us another opportunity to be His ambassadors – willing purveyors of The Good News.

"Boldly, we must seize each opportunity, letting the peace of God rule our hearts and whatsoever we do, do it in His name, humbly giving thanks for another blessed day – another opportunity."

Everyday Miracles

Lord, You work for me a miracle
when You send a helping hand –
to help me through the trials of life
to conquer its demands. . .
a hand for work,
a hand for play,
a hand to help in every way. . .
You grant to me a miracle
when You send Your helping hand.

You send me down a blessing, Lord –
the blessing of Your arms –
You wrap me up in Godly love –
You keep me safe from harm. . .
arms to rock me,
arms to comfort,
arms to keep me warm. . .
another blessed miracle
when You wrap me in Your arms.

You give to me the power of love –
a love like Yours – divine –
a love truly miraculous
unselfish, grand and fine. . .
a love to give
and love returned,
love freely to release. . .
when You give to me Your power of love –

Everyday Miracles

You bestow to me love's peace.

You grant to me, Lord, wisdom –
the miracle of Your way –
how to cope with life's uncertainties,
how to make it day by day. . .
the wisdom of acceptance,
the wisdom to deny,
the wisdom to leave it all to You
and never to ask why.
Yes, You grant me, Lord, Your wisdom
to use it by and by.

Miracles – everyday miracles –
God's wonders from on high!

Proem. . .

<u>Exhale</u>

"You can only hold your breath so long.

"You've flexed and forgiven; you've cringed and you've cried; you've wondered and waited; you've cared without ceasing – you've prodded and pleaded; been battered and broken; suffered in silence; and, you've loved and you've lost.

"You can only hold your breath so long.

"Now, breathe."

Life's Certainty

We've tarried too long
at this fork in the road –
undecided,
hesitant,
scared.
We've stripped down to the quick
all of life's
happiness –
we've instead shattered dreams and tears.

I must carry on
but I'll carry alone –
finally able to breathe
that sigh of relief
for life's one certainty,
and that one certainty is me.

Our things in common
are all
of the past,
and in order to make it
we've had to fake it,
so our futures will differ indeed.
To the east for you;
toward the west for me –
never again
our paths to meet.

Life's Certainty

If there's such a thing
as parting as friends,
we're approaching our last triumph.
As a friend you'll be fine
but you're no man of mine,
just as I'm not the woman
for you.

I'm free!
I'm free!
I'm able to breathe.
I've finally accepted
life's one certainty,
and life's one certainty is me.

Proem. . .

<u>*Be Grateful*</u>

"Have you ever been tempted to say that things just couldn't be worse? Who hasn't. But when the reality of life's frailties hits you, when you remember life five years ago, when you check the mirror and your eyes are dry, when to look at your heart and your scars have healed; then – like the calm before the storm – the burden of your self-pity will be lifted."

Just A Warning

Growing
up hard
is
hard. When
you're forced
to witness,
day after day,
the hard-core
bitterness
that is
status quo
for the
"caged in"
ghetto dwellers,
never once
to be
released –
never once
to enjoy
the peace of
nature's
blessings, then
it's doubly
hard for
one
not to be
somewhat
affected.

This is
just a warning.

Proem. . .

A Bridge Called Love

"Interracial relationships can be scary. We hear things, we read things, we fear the unknown, we retreat. Sometimes, though, one just needs to build a bridge. A bridge can span life's 'valley of differences' and, if set in the right foundation, will withstand any weight, any pressure, any tide that even time cannot."

Ebony Confession

To have captured in a night
that which for generations
had gone unleashed
is in itself a victory, of sorts,
but hollow
in that the bridge,
though built,
has yet to be crossed,
the first step to hesitation lost.

Our meeting of minds
left a semblance of satisfaction
but was stunted from growth
and fell short cause distracted
by a heritage
too close to be denied.

My haunting stare –
your innocent touch,
suspended in time
as we watched unfold
an intercourse of our common goals –
the very shield to this fairy tale untold. . .
'tis best we leave this bridge uncrossed,
the first step to hesitation lost.

Proem. . .

<u>*Change Reaction*</u>

"Sometimes time is just what we need.

"Change comes with time – our hope relies on change."

Survival

For some the sky's
too high
And the sea's
too wet. . .
For them time
holds no hope
For that brighter,
clearer tomorrow.

But we,
we've reached the clouds,
and we've rode life's waves. . .
Thriving one on the other,
believing one in another. . .

Surviving the test of time.

Proem. . .

An Open Letter

"My Love:

"Where to begin with this is difficult. It is difficult because I am attempting to verbalize an entity that heretofore was only a spirit . . . a spirit, I believe, that has always been here. I knew it not, but I felt its presence, and it filled me – as a quiet whisper, a gentle breeze, a hint of light, a muffled cry, a warm embrace. I marvel at this revelation.

"But now, by the grace of God, the spirit has been transformed and, with all the pomp and splendor that life can hold, has manifested itself in the body of a man. And, that man is you.

"I became breathless and remain without adequate words to convey the magnificence and magnitude of this manifestation and how it makes me feel; how my half-moon life is now full circle – shiny and bright – whole and complete. I thank God for the blessing of you.

"I trust in God. He makes no mistakes. And because He allowed you to linger in my whispers, to sway in my breezes, to share my embraces, I trust that God will continue to sustain and enrich this blessing.

"I dare not minimize or trivialize anyone or anything that has gone before. For, all that has come and gone has added to our life's lessons, enhancing the essence of who we are. But, I must accept and acknowledge you for who and what you are to me: the absolute, unconditional, ultimate love of my life!

"Forever yours,"

Simply, I Love You

Black is beautiful,
Great is Ali,
Always is forever;
Life – you and me.

Nothing's fairer than equal,
God is endless as time,
As all these are true;
Simply, I love you.

Proem. . .

The Real Thing

"Many of us are pressured into feeling that we just don't have the time. But, we who are wise take the time.

"For, sometimes the reality of actuality is the only answer. Dreaming or fantasizing just won't do."

Back To Reality

Careful now –
you wouldn't want to hurt
a sweetie pie like me.
Careful now –
as time has proved,
I'm sweet as,
light as,
spicy as
any rich cream pie can be.

Careful now –
watch those arms.
Careful now –
don't squeeze too tight.
For as you know,
I'm fragile as,
dainty as,
can melt as fast
as the first winter snow.

Let us take our time –
the night is young –
moon-gaze awhile –
just take it slow.
Music's low,
light's low,
I'm aglow,
We're having fun –
no need to rush and go.

Back To Reality

Take care with me –
I'm very gentle.
Careful now –
I just might break.
You'll give a bit,
I'll give a bit;
we'll move in time,
at times we'll rhyme.
You've got it now –
just give and take.

For, I love to kiss,
I love to cuddle,
I love to hug,
I love to make love.
Uninhibited –
wild as a storm,
as free as a nude on a bear-skin rug!

Enough of this!
My meandering mind –
yes, to dream is fine,
but I must back a bit and realize
that a dream this is
and no matter how great,
but all I have done is
fantasize.

Proem. . .

Zero Tolerance

"Certain behaviors are just not acceptable. Trying to accept the unacceptable is unacceptable. Though some issues be resolvable – some indiscretions forgiven; though some obstacles are overcome and some broken hearts mended; though time be a healer and God be our guide. . .

"Some things are just not acceptable!"

If The Shoe Fits

I never was able to stand
a man who could not
be a man –
who'd turn on by artificial means –
who'd sniff and
shoot up all his dreams.

Yes, what I say may be rude,
but, I can't stand your altitude.

I never was able to buy
the guy whose place is
ten miles high –
who lives to be one of the crowd –
suspended
in his euphoric cloud.
'Cause how can I look you
eye to eye
when I'm down here
and you're sky high?

Yes, what I say may be rude,
but, I can't stand your altitude.

You say love's blasé –
respect's gone by –
you ask how –
you ask why?

If The Shoe Fits

Know this. . .

I never was able to stand
a man who could not
be a man
and live life to just be him –
not having to be one of them.

Yes, what I say is cold –
but, it's true.
I can't stand them and
I can't stand you. . .

If The Shoe Fits!

Proem. . .

Giving Thanks

"*Over the years, I have, with much concerted effort, tried to pay due homage to what some folk call life's 'small things'. . . the air we breathe, the water we drink, our peace of mind, our portion of health, eyes to see, ears to hear, and warm hearts capable of laughter and love.*

"*I, though, dare not call them small things, for I believe they are made to be small by the meager thanks we give. For, utter magnificence lies in the fact of these gifts and awesome is the Gift Giver.*

"*A little bit of thanks goes a long way, but a lot of thanks is a lot better.*"

Thank You, Lord

I woke this morning
and touched my face
and realized
it was by Thy grace
that my heart still beats
and the sun still shines
and the wind still blows
and the path still winds. . .

And I just want to thank You, Lord.

I looked to the sky
and it still shone blue
the clouds were there
and the grass had dew
and the robins sang
and the church bells rang
and the children played
as the faithful prayed. . .

And I just want to thank You, Lord.

And as I walked
along my daily way
I listened to what
my Lord did say
I set my ears to hear
and my eyes to see

Thank You, Lord

and my heart to obey
my God and not me. . .

And I just want to thank You, Lord, My Lord.

The night did come
as I thought it would
my heart was glad
and my soul felt good
and the stars did glow
and the moon did shine
on another blessed day
for me and mine. . .

And I just want to thank You, Lord.

And we'll sleep the night away
as the faithful pray. . .

Yes, I just want to thank You, Lord.

Proem. . .

No Wonder

"I wonder to this day, and I guess I'll always wonder   was it a boy? was it a girl?   What I don't wonder about is was it a child.

"I not once wondered whose child.   I know the child is mine.   I never wonder where My Child be.   I know My Child be with God.

"I see My Child in my son's face, I hear My Child in my daughter's voice, I feel My Child in my longing soul. . . yet, My Child be with God, with God for goodness' sake.

"It was never an issue of choice, rather a matter of acceptance.

"Yes, My Child be with God and, yes, God is good!

A Minute To Pause

Sorry, Miss,
I know you're only
twenty-six,
but you're going through
The Change.

Puberty to senility
should take
a lifetime.
You've made it there in leaps
and bounds;
shouldn't have taken the
short way round.

Sorry, Miss,
to inform you of this,
but your man's
spring chicken
has suddenly turned
mid-winter
cold.

The Change creates
changes.
Patience is much shorter;
temper tends to fly;
poundage daily rises;
you have the urge to cry.

Minute To Pause

Everything started
ends in a flash –
some just lukewarm,
but,
yet and still a flash.

The hump's
a long ways up
and a short plunge down.
Tis hard to
accept the valley
when you've skipped right over
mountain top.

Sorry, Miss.

Proem. . .

Picking Up The Pieces

"It's a difficult task to try and pick up your own life's shattered and scattered pieces but, fortunately, no one can do it for you. It's fortunate because, if allowed by someone else, you may end up being that someone else's clone, and the you that you so desperately wanted to reassemble may be forever lost to the unrecognizable.

"Alterations, if you choose, but you never want to lose your essence."

Broken

To starve that which has
watered and nurtured you over the
hills and valleys of life
is not lucid.
Life is such that
it must be dealt in priorities –
to be based on those who only know you
in your highest hour
or those
who can only be seen in
light and joy and ecstasy
is most rash.
Replenish those from whom you have
so steadily drained your sap of existence;
replenish,
before love's well runs dry;
lest the unlubricated wheels of life
will come to a screeching
halt.

To feed the externals and
starve the internals?
Life just doesn't work
that way. Love nor life
can grow that way;
yes, 'tis true,
you reap only that that you sow.

Broken

I can face the shattered dreams;
weather the drowned hopes;
even climb from the depths of despair.
But how to face
the memories –
those severing, blinding memories?
I fear in trying to scalpel
the past I may injure tomorrow;
tomorrow,
the only thin thread that keeps me from
attempting to destroy
them both.

After years of faithful uphill climbing
to be suddenly plummeted to the
blatant reality that all is lost,
is trauma in the raw;
so raw that the adage
time healeth all
just can't apply.
So hurt, the wound so deep, that
adding salt makes it pain no more, no less -
just constant,
unwavering, agonizing
truth!

Proem. . .

<u>*Fond Memories*</u>

"Certain memories, I am convinced, are created expressly for the purpose of daydreaming. Oh, the bliss of reminiscing about the quiet excitement of childhood – transcending time and space – adrift back to the place where all was right with the world and its people.

"Remember your first dance? Remember your first car? Remember that first home run and the crowd going wild as they all yelled your name? And, who can forget wedding day, birth of children, Ganny's yeast rolls or Miss Mayfield's fruit trees?

"Each memory is special unto itself, all golden nuggets of the past that when recalled makes one realize how extraordinary life can be.

"Dream on."

The Kiss

I need only
close my eyes –
I need only
to sit still. . .

for the darkness
and the quiet
brings the kiss alive –
renewed. . .

tells the story of a journey
to life's apex –
chaste and pure. . .

imparts freedom
to enjoy
the hope in
many shared tomorrows. . .

grants the refuge
of escape
with each resurgence –
fresh and new. . .

for this kiss, My Love –
sweet, sweet kiss, My Love,
The Kiss, My Love –
is you.

Proem. . .

<u>*Worthy Baggage*</u>

"Some men just don't get it. They just don't realize that our children are a gift from God – they are our reward.

"Some men don't know that women bring to the table of life many gifts – gifts of joy and peace and laughter; gifts of faithfulness and patience and humor; the gift of love and the gift of God's reward.

"Some men don't get the fact that our rewards are their rewards.

"But, thank God, some men do."

Love Me. . . Love My Child

My heart runneth over with an untapped love –
to the brink – not one more drop to be held.
My soul's unrested and my passions run wild –
but if you love me. . . love my child.

When I look to your eyes, it's peace I see.
I envy your lips – that perpetual smile.
You're God's creation and the world should know,
but if you love me. . . love my child.

You're as close to perfection as one would want –
but, the writing's on the wall – if only I'd read.
I tremble, I shake with this thought so vile –
that you love me. . . but not my child.

I'd not sever my hands for my feet to keep
nor forfeit my speech in order to hear.
Time speaks truth – yes, it's been awhile –
Time says, you love me. . . but not my child.

Yes, I've tried to ignore the obvious choices –
beguiled by your charm and manner mild.
I'd give all there is to make it be –
I'd give all of me to make it be –
seems there's nothing I can do to make it be
that you'd love me. . . love my child.

Proem. . .

<u>Don't Settle for Less</u>

"To say it's as good as it gets runs the risk of complacency.

"Let's just say. . . it's as good as it gets until it gets better. That way, you'll always strive to do your best, always strive for more."

Before You Know It

Be cautious,
Dear One, or
before you know it
your fondest dreams will have drifted away;
don't take things for granted or things neglect –
and before you step out
take some time to reflect.

Up-and-at-em,
Dear One, or
before you know it
the goals you've set will be out of reach.
Don't put things off or before you know it
the way you thought paved
will be rocky and rough.

But, not too fast,
Dear One, or
before you know it
you'll have passed your stop and be out of breath.
Take things easy –
wait till the time is right or before you know it
you're too far to come back.

Do aim for the top,
Dear One,
but in doing so
don't step on your neighbor or enemy.
Respect all mankind and before you know it
you'll be the Star among stars
you're destined to be.

Proem. . .

Patent for Passion

"Everybody wants to come up with that big invention, that hot product, that consumer's delight commodity that will enable them to quit their job, help the homeless, rescue the lost and save the whales!

"It would have to be something 'to die for'. . . something you can't do without. . . something heretofore unobtainable. . . .

"Oh, well, good luck!"

Liquid Sensuality

Deliberate
and slow –
I'd flow from
head to toe –
gently lingering,
gladly responding
to the whisper
of your
erotic
cry.

Engulfed
in this
protective glaze,
I'd keep you
totally satisfied –
mind, body
and soul,
warm. . .

If only
sensuality
came in
liquid
form!

Proem. . .

Payback

"When we're hurt, we have a tendency to want to hurt back. There is an inherent danger in this approach to pain because it may start a vicious cycle that requires someone to yell 'uncle,' which creates the distinct possibility that the cycle will never end.

"Have patience. Life – the master of payback – will do the job for you. There will be no need for yelling and no onset of vertigo."

Just Rewards

Pray there will never come a day
when you will really need someone –
someone to tell your troubles to –
to share your downs and help rebound –
someone you know who truly cares. . .
Just pray that day will never come
'cause I will not be there.

I trust I'm not your last resort,
the one you count on when all others fail –
for I'm not that steadfast rock of old –
you've molded me bitter, chilled me cold –
from the meekest of meek to downright bold. . .

So, don't expect too much of me,
I've learned your rules "A" to "Z".

In fact. . .
I'll be where you have been these years –
in training on how to disappear.
I'll turn my back,
clinch my hand,
blank my mind,
close my eyes,
and reappear when all is grand.

So, wherever it was
you happened to be –
look there, you may just find me.

And, even though I still may care –
pray that day will never come
'cause I will not be there.

Proem. . .

<u>*Compulsive Behavior*</u>

"Regarding relationships, it's funny almost that all too often we seem to be attracted to the same type person. Even though we may swear again and again. . . 'in no case,' 'under no circumstances,' 'when hell freezes over,' sooner than not, we're back in the mix (or should I say mess).

"This phenomenon may just have to do with that which is familiar. Oddly enough, there is an inherent comfort found in familiar persons, places and things; but what looks good to us or makes us feel good is not necessarily good for us. And, though this concept is not unfamiliar to us, it is easily forgotten and readily overlooked, particularly during times of passion or in times of stress.

*"It's been said, and no doubt proven, that familiarity can breed contempt. No wonder then that many of these relationships end up the same. The optimum word to note here being **end**.*

"One thing is for sure – it ain't funny."

Inner Thoughts

I feel down –
way down.
What is it? Could it be my heart
is broken? Could it be I've
let myself be hurt again?
Again!
I promised I'd never.
Maybe
it's just indigestion.
I couldn't be that foolish!

It hurts
but I don't remember falling.
Time will surely
ease
my pain, but it mustn't take long
cause I can't take much.
Conditioning
one's
self to feel no pain has surprisingly
turned out to be only
a temporary thing.
I must re-enroll.

Could
it be I was kicked while down? But
I just don't
remember
being that

Inner Thoughts

low.
Whatever,
I got the full treatment.
I ache from top to bottom –
from side to side.
Will it ever end?

I must remember,
I
must!

Could it be in my
anxiousness to
please that I compromised my
beliefs to
the point of
rupturing my morals?
Can it be I strained in
trying to love too
much
too
soon?
Possibly
in my feelings of total
rejection
I re-opened old wounds that I
thought
were forever
closed!

Inner Thoughts

Can this be?

Truly,
I really don't know.

But. . .

I must remember,
I
must –
and soon;
but it mustn't take long
cause I can't take much!

Proem. . .

Drugs

"If not your daughter, then my son. If not my house, then next door. If not next door, then at school. If not at school, then in church.

"It's not here or there – it's here, there and everywhere.

"God bless us all!"

Please, Come In Out Of The Rain

It's raining, raining, raining,
My Dear,
won't you, please, come in –
in out of the rain.
Life's storms are raging
high day and night;
won't you, please, come in –
in out of the rain.

I'm searching, searching, searching,
My Daughter,
won't you, please, come in –
in out of the rain.
My heart feels your pain
as you wander
and tarry;
my soul knows the burden
of hopelessness fraught.

Forgive me – I forgive you –
My Darling, My Child;
won't you, please, come in –
in out of the rain.
Little Girl, Baby Girl,
just take Mommy's hand;
let me help you escape
this deadly rain of fire.

Please, Come In Out Of The Rain

I will dry you, embrace you,
protect, steer and keep you,
just, please, come in –
in out of the rain.
We'll let God be our guide
on this road – share our load –
Honey, please, come in
out of life's angry blast.

God loves you, I love you,
please, hear me –
we love you;
just, please, come in –
in out of the rain.
I beseech you,
Prodigal Daughter, My Dear,
Sweet Daughter, to,
please,
come in out of the rain.

Proem. . .

Less Is More

"Lessening the frills, the fuss and the mess promotes an atmosphere that is more conducive to success.

"Keep it simple."

Plain and Simple

I can't detail my every feeling;
don't ask –
don't think I ever can.
Could be simply that I'm a woman –
could be simply that you're a man.

Some things must strive
left unspoken
so do your best with
between the lines.
Could be simply that I'm a woman –
could be simply you've caught my eye.

Who knows
why I sit and look
from head to toe –
at each strand of hair.
Accept the fact that someone's caring,
and forgive me
if I seem to stare.

You need not know
my every thought;
don't pry,
wouldn't say if I could.
Not all things in life are pleasant
but thoughts of you
are always good.

Plain and Simple

But, this one time
I'll be specific
and let you know
what my heart's made of.
Yes, simply I am a woman,
but, truthfully, I'm a woman in love.

Proem. . .

<u>*Missing Out*</u>

"Fear of rejection can be very debilitating. If you want for something or someone and never try, you may be further crippled by a self-imposed 'what if' curse.

"Being that faith's opposite is doubt and that doubt breeds fear, just have the faith to be yourself – the you God has made you to be. And, if God be for you, then who can win against you. Surely, not fear.

"Go for it."

If Only

If only
I could tell you
just how much you mean to me –
how since you've come into my life,
oh, how my life doth soar, and,
the heights to which you take me,
if only in my dreams,
puts me right atop the world,
if only you could see.

If only
you would read my signs
then you would surely know
the depth, the width, the breadth
and that I love you so, and,
I'd shout it out to all the world –
for all of man to be
a part of this
great love of ours,
if only you would read.

If only
you would take my hand –
if only
I would take your arm –
then we'd be safe forever
from outside hurt or harm.
Embracing we each other –
in total – not in part,
could mend our minds, unite our souls –
and let the love flow free
in our hearts.

Proem. . .

A Dream Come True

"As children, we sometimes have recurrent dreams – dreams of adventure, whimsical dreams, exotic dreams, frightening dreams. The spectrum was endless.

"But, no matter the theme, we'd always awaken to our world of reality – sometimes the very world from which our dreams allowed us to escape.

"Wouldn't it have been nice, though, to have been able to awaken and incorporate our dream life into our real life; of course, interspersing only certain facets – facets of fun and fancy, mystery and magic, laughter and love – picking and choosing images at will, defying basic knowledge of time and space.

"Wouldn't it be nice!"

King Louie – My First

I dreamed you were a King, Dear Lou,
and I, My Lord,
Your Lady. . .
living in the State of Bliss
in a Land called Ecstasy.

This Kingdom it was
free from pain –
the sun shone always – never rain;
a Wonderland void of poverty –
all deemed by you, My Majesty.

One night. . .
you gathered all your subjects –
loyal, true, sublime –
cheering as you declared it law
that I am yours, and you are mine.

Hence,
you bestowed the cherished gifts
of peace, joy and laughter. . .
wished all about a blessed life
and happiness everafter.

We then rode into the sunset –
all throughout eternity. . .
you as My Beloved King,
and I, Your Royal Lady.

Then suddenly I awakened,
my heart overrun with glee.
Yes!
We still live in the State of Bliss
in our Land called Ecstasy.

Proem. . .

Accepting The Charge

*"As believers, we bear the responsibility to share –
particularly to share the comfort found in the blessed
assurance that all of God's promises will be kept.*

*"For those who are wondering and unsure, for those who
are wandering and lost, for those who are drawn to sin and
denounce salvation. . . you must embrace their unbelief.
You must share your joy, share your peace, share the love,
give them hope, and be willing to lead the course.*

*"The mere reflection of your godliness will create light
sufficient for others to find the way.*

"Share your God."

The Prisoner

He searches life's waters
    only to find
    others and pebbles
    just floating in time –
    wandering
    aimlessly,
    anxious,
    suspended,
    but can't find himself
    cause he's locked him inside.

He speaks to the clouds
    and they to him –
    the moon and the stars
    are his best friends –
    looks in the mirror
    and nothing he sees,
    still night turns to day
    but he turns up empty.

Yo-yo's, life, lines on a graph –
    one day bare
    the next overdressed;
    caught in time's whirlwind –
    perched on its crest –
    just look to yourself
    and you'll find Him inside –
    the answer's in God,
    the answer is God.

Proem. . .

<u>Soul Mate</u>

"There is no logical, rational explanation.

"Now that I have found you, there is just an overwhelming sense that I can never do without you – that I have never been without you – a sense that you have always been right here.

"The manifestation of your being fills me."

When We Met

I believe we met
when I first realized
that the breeze of the trees have meaning. . .

I believe we met
when the winds of song
in my soul started singing. . .

I believe we met
when mercy unpacked
and convinced grace to stay. . .

We met, I'm sure,
at the dawning –
when the dark of night turns to light of day. . .

I believe we met
when I passed life's test –
there is no answer to why. . .

I believe we met
with each teardrop –
we meet whene'er I cry. . .

I believe we met
when fear moved out
and peace decided to dwell. . .

We met, I'm sure,
in the stillness –
in the whisper of "all is well."

Proem. . .

"All is fair in love and war. . . and when under the influence of drugs."

An Unfairy Tale

There once was a rapist
the scum of the earth –
lower than none other.
He raped at will –
respected no life –
but he didn't rape his Mother.

I once knew a thief
who'd steal anything;
a "klepto" at best, no less –
from enemies, friends,
neighbors and like
but kept his Mother out of such mess.

A liar's a liar
whose lies can build
from the mini to the stout.
But not to his Mother
the pride of his life,
for her the truth would hold out.

The rapist, the thief,
the liar alike
bear the kinship of brother.
Violate, steal and lie –
yes, they will –
but never, never to Mother!

Proem. . .

I'll Always Miss My Momma

"There is no hurt that compares to the loss of a mother.

"Though I thank God for the gift of her love, the times I and my mother shared, of the images that make me weep, of the memories that make me smile, of the smells that conjure up holiday gatherings, of the certain words and silly jokes that always made her laugh, and of her unheeded advice that I just now am beginning to understand – with all of this and much, much more, I miss my mother still. I miss my mother, and I always will.

"My mother's passing was part of The Master's perfect plan. I accept this. Yet, I cried at her passing, I cry at this writing, and I may even cry tomorrow, but God understands my tears.

"God knows that I know that for the rest of my life that no husband, no son or daughter, no friend, no sister or brother, no aunt, no uncle, no one from my past and no one I will meet can ever replace my mother.

"I'll Always Miss My Momma.

"God understands."

Your Living Was Not In Vain

You leave us, Dear One,
Yes, your time has come
To take your heavenly place,
Amongst the angels above,
Around God's throne and to
Look upon God's face.

Yes, we'll miss you, Dear One,
The joy and the love
That to others you freely did give,
You've been etched in our minds
And will be part of our hearts
For as long as we all shall live.

Our hearts and minds will always remember
The joy you gave, the lives you've touched;
We'll cherish your memory and honor your name –
For us you would do as much.

In times to come when we're alone
We'll treasure deep within our hearts,
The catapult, enriching part
You played in all our lives.

We'll meet again, and soon, Dear One,
Remembering always to try
Not to let one day go by
Without sweet thoughts of you.

So, rest peaceful, Dear One,
For you're now free from
Life's troubles, life's strife, life's pain –

Your Living Was Not In Vain

We just want you to know that we love you so,
and that
Your living was not in vain.

Proem. . .

<u>Poor Visits Poverty</u>

"It seems in life that the lives we live are never quite good enough. We always want for more – greener pastures, higher heights, deeper depths, whiter whites. We all are guilty. We all have been there.

"But, when you journey into life and witness its magnitude and are blessed by its wisdom, then all that's to be said is, 'Thanks be to God.'

> *"'Thank God for your crust of bread*
> *And thank Him for the jelly jar.*
> *Thank God for your soleless shoes*
> *And thank Him for your run-down car.'*

"Thank God!"

But I've Never Seen a Mountain

I've felt the bite of hunger –
The hollowness of loneliness –
Known suicides by the score,
But, I've never seen a mountain.

I've seen the paint peel off the walls –
I've smelled the stench of pee-stained halls –
Come close to death and wished I'd died,
But, I've never seen a mountain.

I've seen good women hit the streets
To clothe and feed their loved ones –
Seen drunks in gutters fast asleep,
But, I've never seen a mountain.

But, I've read of mountains high, so high –
I've dreamed of lily cluttered fields –
I've imagined I've soothed life's every ache
In the streams of my magic mountain.

Oh, yes, I realize that rats must eat –
That roaches too must have a home –
I know my dream's all selfishness,
But, my dream's to see that mountain.

Yet, it's only dawned on me of late
That what I have need not be destiny
But what I have, I'd gladly give
Just for once to see that mountain.

Proem. . .

<u>*Reflections*</u>

"From time to time, we all need to take a break – a mental health day – to assess ourselves within ourselves. We need that quiet, private time to rediscover who we are and what we are doing – to review in our minds what it is that makes us tick. We need to reexamine our past and learn from it – we need to make plans for our future, remaining flexible and receptive to change. Too, we must realize that our present is ever upon us and that we live the consequences of our past decisions – good or bad.

"But, none of this does any good – an exercise in futility – if we are not open and honest.

"Remember always – to thine own self be true!"

Diary Page 79

Dear Diary–

Happiness is a wonderful thing.

Though today, Diary, I am happy, I feel sad – sad in that one so humble as myself can be *so* happy while the world around is in such a hectic state: the ugliness and hatred of war; the injustice of injustice; poverty and starvation; parentless children, childless couples; man's indifference to man; and the senseless pervasiveness of prejudice when there need not be any at all.

Why, Diary, happiness for me but not happiness for all?

Yes, happiness is truly a wonderful thing and though today I am truly happy. . . I wonder.

Proem. . .

In All Probability

"If you wonder whether a thing is for real, it probably isn't. If you suspect that it won't work, your suspicion is probably sound. If you just don't understand, it's probably incomprehensible.   If we're speaking here of men, you know I'm probably right!"

And Now You're Gone

You came into my life
like a spring, pre-dawn rain
falling ever so gently
soothing where it hurt
cleansing ever so deeply
washing 'way the pain
and I never questioned why
just was glad that you came.

You brought with you the premise
that life is to be lived
as you guided with precision
this eager, uncaged bird
on a flight of joy and magic
to heights unknown, undreamed
you gave to my life hope
and, yes, I believed.

I trusted in your premise
to live not just exist
I gloried in your promise
that you'd always be the one
still I believed in my mind
that you wouldn't stay long
now I feel it in my heart
yes, 'tis true –
and now you're gone.

Proem. . .

Pity Party

"Thanks be to our God that, at times, we may get lonely but we are never, never alone!

"Our promise from God fulfilled."

Too Bad You Had To Leave Again

Gee, too bad you had to miss
The drapes whispering wearily
Their hating to just hang around –
Too bad you had to leave again.

More than that you had to miss
The sniggles of contented chair
As I gave a leg massage –
Too bad you had to miss the fun.

Sorry you missed the baffled bed
Explaining of her tiredness
Apparently from lack of sleep –
Too bad you had to leave again.

Up and spoke the grieving floor
Complaining of the heavy load
And splinters in his every joint –
Too bad you had to hit the road.

At last horned in complaining couch
The agony of aching arms
From a many pointed elbow –
Too bad you had to leave again.

Then to top the evening off
I confidentially asked of me
Ways to rid the company –
Too bad you had to leave again!

Proem. . .

<u>Taken By Surprise</u>

"It can be intimidating to be drawn out of one's emotional comfort zone...drawn by the power of a stranger's smile, by the lull of the stranger's voice, by the touch of the stranger's hand, by the gleam in this stranger's eyes.

"Don't be intimidated. Be glad. Imagine you've returned the favor.

"For, you are strangers no more."

Unbridled Blush. . .

That body-all blush that

transforms temperate blood

into a fiery, tempestuous river

so rushing,

so inundating,

flowing with such vehemence

that its mere velocity

is capable of making

the most ardent disbeliever

yield to the pleasures

of having the world

move in one's hand. . .

ain't life grand!

Proem. . .

I Believe

"'Then came the disciples to Jesus apart, and said, Why could not we cast him out?

"'And Jesus said unto them, Because of your unbelief: for verily I say unto you, If ye have faith as a grain of mustard seed, ye shall say unto this mountain, Remove hence to yonder place; and it shall remove; and nothing shall be impossible unto you.'"

Matthew 17:19-20

Prayer Of Faith

O, Holy and Gracious Father,
I thank You for the
faith to believe
that through You
all things are possible.

I thank You for a faith
that can conquer the seen
and the unseen –
the known and the unknown.

I thank You for a faith
that knows
when I ask in Your name
and for Your sake
that it will be given.

I thank You for a faith
that is constant,
steadfast and
immovable.

With faith I pray.

Amen.

Proem. . .

<u>Heart-free</u>

"A couple of failed relationships can lend itself to a future dedicated to 'never again' – never again to be vulnerable, never again to put one's heart at risk. One never again wants to experience the aftermath of love lost.

"But, be careful. Developing a heart-free relationship all too often leads to being heartless. Heartless meaning cruel in its crudest sense."

Fair Warning

If ever I should tease you
and tell you
I am yours,
please know that I am teasing;
for I'm forever wrapped within myself,
entrapped,
dead-locked within myself –
never wanting to be free –
satisfied
with a caged-in me.

If ever I should say
I'm staying,
if only till tomorrow,
please know that I am leaving;
for I'd never, never
chance the pain –
to be caught out in the thunder and rain –
believe me,
I wouldn't,
never again.

If ever I should give in
and you think
that you're about to win –
consider yourself the loser;
for I'd never
even play the game –
not to have you uproot my heart,

Fair Warning

rip it,
shred it,
and tear it apart –
no, Sirree, no not me.

 Dreading the past may repeat,
I'll stay steadfast right here,
My Sweet.
Fearful of a
self-hanging,
I'll be safe instead of sorry cause
I choke if I even
tug on this noose –
why should I even try get loose.

So,
if ever I should tease you,
please,
know that I am teasing.

Proem. . .

<u>Coming To Grips</u>

"It's over. The fat lady has sang and gone home. It's finished. The final act is complete, bows have been taken and the curtains drawn. It's ended. There is nothing left to do – there is nothing left to say. Vows of love, honor and obedience have been annulled."

I Accept

My life's taking a sharp turn –
a turn long overdue.
This near-circle's taken my best years;
can't afford going back now –

I accept the change.

There's relative calmness in my days –
a little sleep in my nights –
a relaxing of the mind –
a cleansing of the soul –
less changing of the moods –
a joy in growing old.

I accept the change.

This serenity I've gained
I'm not willing to relinquish.
If alone and serene are two
then alone and serene am I.

And I accept the change.

I Accept

To be alone
does not mean loneliness;
for I intend not to be lonely.
For,
whatever I have,
whatever I do,
wherever I go,
whatever I choose –
be it good or bad,
stop or go,
empty or full,
fast or slow –
whatever it be,
it will be me –

And I accept the change.

I'll never lean
to the point of depending –
I'll only trust
to the point of aching –
I'll love
till the pain starts
and confiding I'll do not at all.

And I accept this change.

I Accept

  There will be no more full circles
and no more tears from me –
for,
I'll never again get raw
to the core
to let another man,
any man,
strip me of my heart,
my soul –
Never, ever again,
ever again!

I'd rather be hard, cold and alone
than naked and vulnerable!

This truly is a change
and I truly do accept!

Proem. . .

Thinking Ahead

"We start early in life daydreaming about the man or woman we will one day marry. We develop a mental picture of their physical attributes and draft a laundry list of mandatory characteristics. . . must be patient, kind, compassionate, intelligent, respectful, loyal and, of course, have a good sense of humor.

"What's amazing is that if we were to compare lists – male to female – they'd read practically the same. What does this tell us? It's a testimony to the fact that we humans have much more in common than we have differences and that which attracts two together need not be expressed by a string of descriptive words.

"One word will do. . . love."

Man Of My Dreams

I met a man – a kind man
the kind of man who understands
the power of the listening ear
the magic of a needed hug
who knows the world revolves on love –
O, Lord, I must be dreaming!

I met a man – compassion's man
a man who judges others not
a kindred soul of truth and light
who consents to live and let live
who's wise enough of heart to forgive –
O, Lord, I must be dreaming!

I met a man – a patient man
a man who seems to comprehend
the intricacies of life and living
accepts my passionate need for giving
let's me be me – what a feeling –
O, Lord, I must be dreaming.

I kissed this man – this gentle man
this gentle man – he kissed me, then
we suffered our hearts to skip a beat
we felt the world move in our hands
now know at last that life is grand –
Yes, Lord, I must be dreaming!

Proem. . .

<u>Detour</u>

"That's it. That's exactly it!

"It's like traveling down a familiar road and then, all of a sudden, you approach a warning sign. The sign says: 'DANGER – FALLING OBJECTS – PROCEED AT YOUR OWN RISK.'

"Tell me. Would you proceed ahead and take the risk of harm, or would you go the long way around, heading for the safety of home? You do know, though, the real risk here is never being able to go back home.

"Don't chance it. Home is where your heart is."

Reunited

Sweet chirping birds
and predawn mist
were ecstatic just to witness
the ambush,
capture,
and total control
of two lost but reunited souls.

And as your lips enveloped mine,
and your nomadic tongue
wove its way through the moistness
of my consenting mouth –
were it not for
the hour
of that misty morn
and the generosity
of your unselfishness,
I'd have been a prisoner
of my own untamed,
unchained,
memories.

Proem. . .

Dynamic Duo

your melody – beats to the tune of my heart;
your harmony – touches my longing soul;
your strumming – soothes my troubled mind;
your rhythm – gently rocks my world;
you're my boy and I'm your girl!

<u>Music And You. . .</u>

That explosive

combination

capable of blasting

into the Pandora's Box

of my inner emotions –

to release

hidden passions

thought forever

pent up in me,

setting my

cramped

soul free,

letting me live,

at last!

Proem. . .

<u>We All Need Balance</u>

"A relationship that only functions when one party has the tendency to always give way to the other party is a dangerous relationship. It voids itself of equality – leaving a lop-sided, off-kilter kinship that may, at times, exist; but, because it lacks balance, will never really live.

"The remedy. . . allow respect to reside – respect, life's great equalizer."

Submissive

I guess I'll have to try once more
to start a new beginning;
here I don't seem to be winning –
here mine's not even my own.

I'm now freed to the seas again and
whether steady afloat or unsure –
I'll expect nothing less and nothing more
than self-confidence. . . and that on loan.

I'll not put all my eggs in one basket –
I fear the cholesterol –
To be burnt from the inside out
can surely take its toll.

Totality's the price I've paid
just to come up empty-handed –
still flat on my face I've landed;
no longer will I play this role.

For to be held while already down
was your idea of a mercy killing.
Why not – when I was so willing
to gulp thrice twice and drown.

Proem. . .

<u>*But. . .*</u>

"Excepting.. . bar... without... excluding... yet... save... still... unless... nevertheless... however... though... conversely... lacking... until... if... and the list goes on and on – and so does time."

"I Love You, But..."

I know
you
love me,
but...
but,
your but's
in the
way!

Proem. . .

<u>Root Of All Evil</u>

"We all know at least one, if not several persons, who define themselves by what they have materially. Sadly, they equate who they are with those little pieces of green paper and foolishly this is where they place their hope. They seem to be duped by a false sense of security but will find, in due time, that this disingenuous security will ultimately fail them.

"Better they should fill their storehouses with life's true riches – good works, righteousness, godliness, faith, love, patience, meekness – those things forever and eternal. Keys, one and all, to happiness."

Man-In-The-Box

How does it feel
to stand there bare –
exposed to the world,
a specimen rare;
stripped of respect,
a man out of luck,
so expertly cleaned
not a hair's left to pluck?

Is it worth that
two hundred grand a year
to live your life
in constant fear?
To sacrifice soul and dignity
is one compromise
I just can't see.
To me a man's thoughts
should be tax free!

I just thank God it's you
and not "minimum wage" me!

Proem. . .

<u>Commitment</u>

"When referring to relationships, the 'C' word has been given a pretty bad rap. Of late, it's being bantered about as having this negative connotation, synonymous with words like fear and uncertainty.

"Certainly, we would all be better off if we'd just stick to Webster's definition – 'a pledge or promise to do something.'

"Now, is that anything to be afraid of? Just think about it. If you're afraid of commitment, you're afraid of the truth, and if you're afraid of the truth, you'll never be free. . . never free to honor your pledges or keep your promises – never free to fulfill your commitments."

No Matter What!

Having
thought I may have
lost you has made
me realize
that no matter what
the price, or wherever you
may be, I'll set aside life's
pomp and majesty,
for,
I will always love you.

I'll question not your
motives, take
all the time you
need.
Whether a mountain
you have to cross,
or the world you
have to see –
reality you'll always
find in me and,
yes,
I'll always love you.

You've been my solace –
you've been my comfort
a
thousand
times and more.

No Matter What!

At times I've been
a burden
a nuisant albatross –
 in this deal
you've surely lost,
but,
remember
I'll always love you.

I just want you to know if you need me
you can count on me
being
right here.
Despite my shortcomings, my
tendency to refrain;
rest assured
I'll forever remain
the one
who will always love you.

Proem. . .

<u>*My Genesis 1*</u>

"God said it!

It is so!

It is good!

And God blessed them."

Simply Put

Intellectually, it would be a wise thing for us to emotionally
prepare for one day being without each other.
But, because we —

awaken...together

breathe...together

sleep...together

eat...together

cry...together

sing...together

work...together

pray...together

care...together

soothe...together

err...together

smile...together

share...together

think...together

grow...together

survive...together

hurt...together

listen...together

dance...together

play...together

connect...together

need...together

and

love each other

then, simply put, we'll just have to

live and love

together...forever!

Proem. . .

<u>*Invasion Of Your Privacy*</u>

"I love to watch you while you sleep.

"In the quiet of night, it seems as though I can actually hear your heartbeat – sweet, sweet music to my ears.

"I bear witness to the flutter of your eyes and imagine that you're dreaming dreams of me – pleasant dreams – dreams of always and forever.

"I steal kisses – soft, gentle kisses. . . from your brow, your nose, your cheek, your chin – comfy kisses to keep you through the night.

"I feel the strength of a soul at rest, as your body lay next to mine – our body to body, our soul to soul.

"Peace be with you the morrow, My Love."

Breathless

Your eyes –
windows to your world;
revealing nothing –
telling all.

Your heart –
powerful and strong;
rooted and righteous –
understanding weakness.

Your mind –
instant, constant truth;
in the ease of day –
in midnight's eerie shadows.

Your soul –
soulful and loving;
reflective of God –
resting in hallowed peace.

The purity
of your clarity
leaves me
breathless.

Proem. . .

<u>The Inevitable</u>

"Death is as much a part of life as birth. Depending upon life's circumstances, we may, in fact, die a thousand deaths. But, there is an end to life, that point where we cease to be, that moment when the nostrils into which God breathed the breath of life will breathe no more.

"A soul transformed."

Final Wishes

I have come here to state
that when I die
that there be no wake for me
where mourners sit and cry.

Just take me to the graveyard
and lower me in the ground
grieve for me if you please
but no, no whimpering sound.

And as I lay there hushed and cold
just pray the Lord to bless my soul.

My Prayer

Humble me,
O, Lord,
in the likeness of
Thy great teacher, John.
Grant me the continued knowledge
that Thou art
the light that illuminates,
the bread that sustains,
the water that cleanses –
not only in my life, Lord,
but for all mankind
throughout the world.
I give to you the glory.
Glory be to Thee,
O, Lord,
Most High.

Amen.

(Matthew 3:13-15)

In Conclusion. . .

To write an ending when I am not yet finished is a challenge, for life goes on for me.

Truly, I feel I have come full circle but, no doubt, this sense of completion just represents my first go-around. For, I believe there are many more hills to climb. There will be new deadlines to meet – new faces to greet; more problems to solve – more needs to be met; there will be new territory and old ground; hands to be held – bad habits to break; many lessons to learn, and much love to give. . . all bits and pieces that when linked together will form the substance from which life's circles are created.

As I start my new circle, I start happy – very, very happy. For I look back on a blessed life and look forward to the same. . . because I know that the God that has kept me thus far will be the God who will forever sustain me. I find comfort in this blessed assurance.

So, as I continue to listen to God's still, sure voice – as I continue to follow His lead – perhaps we will meet again, you and I – perhaps I will see you around the bend.

You now know me well – just call me friend.

About The Author. . .

Marilyn Dean is a lover of life and poetry and has expressed herself through this medium since early childhood.

Marilyn is an empty-nester, having raised two children, most of the time as a single parent. She lives in suburban Chicago, works a nine-to-five and looks forward to being able to travel and to devote more time to her writings and her loved ones.

Marilyn's day-to-day consists not only of life's expected peaks and valleys, but also of twists and turns, of fast forward and reverse, of falling and flying, of ecstasy and pain, of feast and famine, and of half moons and full circles. Having written *"My Story. . . My Way–Living Life Full Circle"* has given her a sense of peace and completion; one circle complete – another circle begun.

Comments are welcome at MQLTD@PRODIGY.NET.